# Navigating the Digital Playground

# Navigating the Digital Playground

Edna Murray

# CONTENTS

| VI | –

# When to Introduce Children to Technology

## Understanding developmental milestones

Understanding developmental milestones is crucial for parents and caregivers as they navigate the complexities of introducing technology to young children. Developmental milestones serve as benchmarks for assessing a child's growth in various areas, including cognitive, social, emotional, and physical development. Familiarizing oneself with these milestones allows parents to better understand their child's readiness for technology use and to make informed decisions regarding screen time, educational apps, and digital tools that align with their developmental stage.

For toddlers, the focus is primarily on sensory exploration and the development of fine motor skills. At this stage, children are naturally curious and engage with their environment through touch and movement. When considering technology, parents can introduce age-appropriate apps that encourage exploration and creativity while ensuring that screen time is limited and balanced with physical play. Tools that promote fine motor skills, such as interactive touch screens or simple games, can be beneficial, but should complement rather than replace hands-on activities.

As children transition into preschool age, they begin to develop social skills and a greater understanding of language. This is an opportune time to introduce educational apps that foster language development, problem-solving, and social interaction. Parents should look for programs that encourage collaboration and communication, allowing children to play and learn together. Maintaining a balance between screen time and outdoor play is essential during this phase, as physical activity supports overall development and helps children learn to manage their emotions and interactions with peers.

In elementary school, children are more capable of understanding rules and boundaries. This is the ideal time for parents to set clear guidelines around technology use, including the amount of screen time allowed and the types of content that are appropriate. Introducing digital literacy skills becomes important at this stage, as children begin to engage with more complex technology and social media. Parents can facilitate discussions about online safety, responsible behavior, and the impact of technology on their social lives. By actively participating in their child's technology use, parents can help cultivate a healthy relationship with digital tools.

Understanding these developmental milestones not only aids in selecting the right technologies but also enhances family bonding activities. Engaging with technology together can provide valuable opportunities for learning and connection. Whether it's exploring educational games or creating digital art as a family, technology can enrich relationships when used mindfully. By keeping developmental milestones in mind, parents and caregivers can navigate the digital landscape more effectively, ensuring that technology serves as a positive force in their child's growth and development.

## Signs of readiness for tech exposure

Recognizing the signs of readiness for tech exposure in young children is crucial for parents, caregivers, and educators. Each child develops at their own pace, and understanding when a child is ready to engage with technology can help ensure that their experiences are both beneficial and age-appropriate. Signs of readiness can manifest in a child's curiosity about devices, their ability to follow instructions, and their social interactions. By observing these behaviors, adults can make informed decisions about when and how to introduce technology.

One clear sign of readiness is a child's curiosity about technology and how it works. If a child shows interest in watching others interact with devices, such as tablets, smartphones, or computers, it may indicate that they are eager to learn. This curiosity can be a natural gateway to introducing educational apps or interactive games that promote learning. Moreover, when children begin to ask questions about technology or express a desire to try it, it can be an opportunity to foster their interest in a structured and supportive way.

Another indicator of readiness is a child's ability to follow basic instructions and respond to prompts. If a child can understand and execute simple commands, such as "press this button" or "swipe here," they may be ready to engage with technology in a more meaningful way. This skill is essential, as it allows children to interact with educational tools effectively, ensuring that they can navigate apps or games designed to enhance their learning experience. Parents and caregivers can encourage this readiness by providing clear guidelines and support during initial tech exposure.

Social interactions also play a significant role in determining a child's readiness for technology. If a child demonstrates the ability to share, take turns, and engage in cooperative play with peers, it can indicate a readiness for more interactive tech experiences. Introducing technology in a collaborative context, such as playing educational games together or using apps that promote teamwork, can help children develop important social skills while enjoying the benefits of technology. Encouraging discussions about their experiences with tech can further enhance their understanding and social development.

Lastly, parents and caregivers should evaluate a child's emotional responses to technology. Signs of frustration or withdrawal when faced with tech challenges may suggest that the child is not yet ready for certain types of exposure. Conversely, children who display excitement and engagement with technology are more likely to benefit from its educational potential. By monitoring these emotional cues, adults can adjust their approach, ensuring that tech exposure is a positive experience rather than a source of stress or anxiety.

In conclusion, recognizing the signs of readiness for tech exposure involves observing a child's curiosity, ability to follow instructions, social interactions, and emotional responses. By taking the time to assess these aspects, parents, babysitters, teachers, and childcare givers can make informed choices about when and how to introduce technology to young children. This thoughtful approach can help create a balanced and enriching digital experience that supports healthy development and learning.

## Recommended age ranges for different technologies

When introducing technology to children, it is essential to consider age-appropriate guidelines that align with their developmental stages. For toddlers aged 0-2, it is generally recommended to limit screen time significantly. At this stage, the focus should be on real-world interactions, such as reading books, engaging in sensory play, and fostering communication skills. If technology is introduced, it should be in the form of interactive tools that encourage physical activity and creativity, rather than passive consumption. Parents can explore apps that promote music or simple cause-and-effect games, ensuring that technology complements rather than replaces hands-on experiences.

As children enter the preschool age range of 3-5 years, there is more flexibility in technology use, particularly with educational content. Research supports the idea that high-quality educational apps can enhance learning when used in moderation. During this period, technology can serve as a valuable resource for enhancing literacy and numeracy skills. Interactive storytelling apps and games designed to teach basic math concepts can be beneficial. It is crucial, however, for caregivers to co-view with children, guiding them through the content and facilitating discussions about what they are learning.

For school-aged children between 6-12 years, technology can play a significant role in both education and socialization. This age group is ready to engage with more complex digital tools, including educational software and online learning platforms. Parents should encourage the exploration of technology that reinforces academic skills and fosters creativity, such as coding games or art applications. Setting clear boundaries for screen time, balancing it with outdoor play and family activities, becomes vital to ensure that children do not become overly reliant on screens for entertainment and social interaction.

In the tween years, ages 10-12, children become more independent and may begin to explore social media and communication platforms. At this age, it is essential for parents to discuss the implications of online interactions and the importance of digital citizenship. Parents should set rules regarding social media use, including privacy settings and appropriate online behavior. Engaging tweens in conversations about their online experiences helps them navigate the complexities of digital communication and fosters an environment of trust and openness.

Throughout all these stages, it is crucial for caregivers to monitor and guide technology use. Establishing family rules around technology—such as designated screen-free times and spaces—can encourage a healthy balance. Additionally, promoting technology that enhances family bonding, such as collaborative gaming or educational projects, can create shared experiences that deepen relationships. By remaining actively involved in their children's technology use, parents and caregivers can cultivate a positive digital environment that supports healthy development and learning.

# 2

# Age-Appropriate Technology Use for Toddlers

## Types of technology suitable for toddlers

When considering technology suitable for toddlers, it is essential to focus on tools that are designed specifically for their developmental stage. Educational toys that incorporate technology, such as interactive learning tablets or smart toys that promote problem-solving skills, can be excellent choices. These devices typically feature engaging visuals, sound, and tactile interactions that capture a toddler's attention while facilitating learning. It is important to select products that are age-appropriate and foster exploration and creativity, ensuring that technology serves as a complement to traditional play rather than a replacement.

Apps designed for toddlers can also provide valuable learning opportunities. Many educational apps focus on basic skills such as counting, letter recognition, and vocabulary building. When choosing apps, seek out those that emphasize interactive learning and avoid passive consumption. Look for applications that encourage active participation, such as those requiring children to solve puzzles or complete tasks. Additionally, consider apps that have been developed in collaboration with educators to ensure they align with early childhood learning goals.

Incorporating technology into a toddler's life should not come at the expense of physical activity and outdoor play. It is critical to establish a balanced approach that includes ample time for free play outside. Parents and caregivers should aim to create a daily routine that allows for both screen time and hands-on experiences, as outdoor play promotes physical health and social skills. Setting specific limits on screen time can help ensure that technology is used thoughtfully, allowing toddlers to develop well-rounded skills in various areas of their lives.

Technology can also play a role in early childhood education settings. Interactive whiteboards, educational videos, and simple coding games can enhance learning experiences in the classroom. These tools can make abstract concepts more tangible for young learners, helping them to grasp ideas through visual and auditory means. Teachers and childcare providers should integrate technology in ways that support the curriculum and engage children in meaningful activities, ensuring that it enhances rather than distracts from learning objectives.

Lastly, teaching toddlers about technology should include discussions about its role in family bonding. Families can engage in activities together, such as watching educational programs, playing interactive games, or exploring apps that promote collaboration. By using technology as a shared experience, caregivers can model healthy interactions and encourage children to communicate and collaborate effectively. This approach not only fosters learning but also strengthens family relationships, making technology a positive force in the lives of young children.

## Guidelines for limiting screen time

Establishing guidelines for limiting screen time is essential for fostering healthy tech habits in young children. One of the most effective strategies is to set clear and consistent time limits based on the child's age and developmental stage. For toddlers, the American Academy of Pediatrics recommends no screen time other than video chatting. For preschoolers, parents can gradually introduce short, high-quality educational content, ensuring that screen time does not exceed one hour per day. Creating a family media plan can help everyone understand when and how technology will be used, promoting a balanced approach to screen time.

In addition to setting limits, it is crucial to prioritize high-quality content over quantity. Parents and caregivers should carefully select educational apps and programs that promote active engagement rather than passive consumption. Tools that encourage creativity, problem-solving, and critical thinking are particularly beneficial for preschoolers. Regularly reviewing and updating the media choices will ensure that children are exposed to the most enriching experiences available, reinforcing the idea that not all screen time is created equal.

Balancing screen time with outdoor play and physical activities is another vital aspect of these guidelines. Encouraging children to engage in activities outside the digital world helps develop their social skills, creativity, and physical health. Families can make this easier by scheduling regular outdoor play sessions or family activities that do not involve screens. This balance fosters a well-rounded development and teaches kids to appreciate both digital and real-world experiences.

Modeling healthy screen habits is also important for young children. Parents and caregivers can demonstrate appropriate technology use by limiting their own screen time during family interactions and prioritizing face-to-face communication. Engaging in tech-related activities together, such as playing educational games or using apps that promote learning, can help children see technology as a tool for collaboration and bonding rather than isolation. This modeling reinforces the idea that technology can enhance relationships when used thoughtfully.

Finally, open communication about technology use is essential in setting boundaries. Encouraging children to express their feelings about screen time and discussing the benefits and drawbacks of technology can promote digital literacy. Teaching kids to recognize when they have had enough screen time and helping them find alternative activities empowers them to make healthier choices. By fostering a supportive environment that values dialogue and understanding, parents and caregivers can successfully navigate the digital playground while ensuring their children thrive in both virtual and real-world settings.

## Interactive vs. passive technology experiences

Interactive technology experiences engage children in meaningful ways, allowing them to actively participate in learning and play. For example, educational apps designed for toddlers often incorporate touch interfaces that enable young children to manipulate objects on screen, fostering fine motor skills and cognitive development. These interactive experiences can encourage problem-solving, creativity, and critical thinking, as children navigate through games and activities that require them to make decisions and see the consequences of their actions in real time. In this sense, interactive technology serves as a dynamic tool that can complement traditional learning methods.

In contrast, passive technology experiences, such as watching television or videos, generally provide less engagement. While these activities can still offer some educational value, they often do not require the same level of active participation from children. Passive experiences may limit opportunities for children to develop essential skills like communication and collaboration, as they are primarily observers rather than active participants. This distinction is crucial for parents and caregivers to understand, as it highlights the need for a balanced approach that prioritizes interactive experiences over passive consumption.

Introducing interactive technology at an early age can set the foundation for positive learning habits. Research suggests that children who engage with interactive screens tend to exhibit better attention spans and greater interest in learning compared to those who primarily experience passive content. Parents can enhance these benefits by selecting age-appropriate educational tools that promote interaction. It is essential to curate a collection of apps and games that not only entertain but also challenge children to think, create, and explore the world around them.

Balancing screen time with outdoor play is equally important in fostering a healthy developmental environment. While interactive technology can provide valuable learning opportunities, it should not replace physical activity or social interaction. Encouraging children to engage in outdoor play allows them to develop their physical skills and social bonds, which are critical during early childhood. Parents can create a daily routine that incorporates both interactive technology and outdoor experiences, ensuring that children benefit from the best of both worlds.

Finally, teaching children about the differences between interactive and passive technology experiences can promote digital literacy from an early age. By guiding children to understand the impact of their choices regarding technology use, parents and caregivers can empower them to make informed decisions as they grow. Encouraging discussions about their favorite apps and activities can help children articulate their thoughts and feelings about technology, fostering a sense of agency and responsibility. As they learn to navigate the digital landscape, children will be better equipped to harness technology's potential while developing critical skills for the future.

# 3

# Balancing Screen Time and Outdoor Play

## Importance of physical activity

Physical activity plays a crucial role in the overall development of young children, serving as a foundation for both physical health and cognitive growth. In an era where technology often dominates children's lives, it is vital for parents, babysitters, teachers, and childcare givers to recognize the importance of incorporating regular physical activity into daily routines. Engaging in outdoor play and physical exercise not only contributes to a child's physical well-being but also enhances their social skills, emotional resilience, and ability to focus, which are essential in a technology-driven world.

Research indicates that children who participate in regular physical activity exhibit improved attention spans and cognitive function. As they explore their environment through active play, they develop critical thinking skills, problem-solving abilities, and creativity. These experiences are invaluable, especially when balanced with technology use. By encouraging children to be physically active, caregivers can help nurture a well-rounded development that complements the educational benefits of age-appropriate technology.

Moreover, establishing a routine that includes outdoor play and physical activities can serve as a natural counterbalance to screen time. This balance is crucial in preventing the negative effects associated with excessive technology use, such as sedentary behavior and social isolation. Parents should aim to model healthy habits by participating in physical activities alongside their children, turning exercise into a fun, shared experience that reinforces family bonding. This approach not only fosters a love for physical activity but also cultivates strong relationships and communication skills within the family.

In addition to health benefits, physical activity can enhance children's social interactions. Group games and team sports provide opportunities for children to learn important social skills such as co-operation, sharing, and conflict resolution. These skills are vital as children navigate their relationships both on and offline. When technology is introduced, children with strong social skills are better equipped to engage positively in digital environments, making them more resilient against issues such as cyberbullying and social media pressures.

Ultimately, prioritizing physical activity in conjunction with technology use creates a holistic approach to child development. By emphasizing the importance of outdoor play and exercise, parents and caregivers can ensure that children develop not only their physical capabilities but also their emotional and social skills. This balanced approach prepares young children to navigate the digital playground with confidence and resilience, setting them up for a healthier, more fulfilled life as they grow.

## Creating a balanced schedule

Creating a balanced schedule for technology use in young children requires careful consideration of their developmental needs and the diverse benefits technology can offer. Establishing a routine that integrates screen time with other activities can create a harmonious environment that promotes learning and healthy growth. By ensuring that technology does not overshadow essential experiences such as outdoor play, creative pursuits, and family interactions, caregivers can foster a well-rounded approach to digital engagement.

To begin crafting a balanced schedule, it is essential to define clear time limits for screen usage. The American Academy of Pediatrics provides guidelines suggesting that children aged two to five should be limited to one hour of high-quality programming each day. This timeframe allows for meaningful engagement with educational content while ensuring that children have ample opportunity to explore the world around them. By setting specific times for technology use, parents and caregivers can help children develop an understanding of moderation and the importance of other activities.

Incorporating outdoor play and physical activity into the daily routine is crucial for a child's overall development. Research indicates that outdoor play contributes significantly to physical health, social skills, and cognitive development. By designating specific times for outdoor exploration, caregivers can encourage children to engage with their environment, enhancing their creativity and problem-solving skills. Balancing technology with nature and physical activity creates an enriching experience that supports holistic growth.

Educational apps and tools can be integrated into the schedule in a way that complements traditional learning. Selecting age-appropriate applications that align with the child's interests and developmental milestones can enhance their learning experience. For instance, interactive storytelling apps can be paired with reading time, while math games can be introduced alongside hands-on activities involving counting and sorting. This synergy between technology and tactile experiences reinforces the learning objectives and keeps children engaged.

Finally, it is vital to include family bonding activities within the balanced schedule. Engaging in technology together, such as playing educational games or watching informative programs, can strengthen relationships while teaching digital literacy. By modeling appropriate technology use, parents and caregivers can guide children in navigating the digital landscape responsibly. Regular discussions about online safety, screen time limits, and the value of face-to-face interactions foster a healthy attitude toward technology and its role in family life.

## Encouraging outdoor play in a tech-heavy world

Encouraging outdoor play in a tech-heavy world is essential for the holistic development of children. In today's society, where screens dominate leisure time, it is crucial to promote the benefits of outdoor activities. Outdoor play not only enhances physical health but also fosters creativity, problem-solving skills, and social interactions among peers. Creating a balanced routine that includes ample outdoor playtime can help counteract the sedentary lifestyle associated with excessive screen time.

To successfully encourage outdoor play, parents and caregivers can set specific times during the day dedicated solely to outdoor activities. This helps establish a routine that prioritizes physical movement and exploration. Activities such as nature walks, playing in local parks, or participating in organized sports provide children with opportunities to engage with their environment. Additionally, incorporating family outings that emphasize outdoor experiences can strengthen bonds while promoting a love for nature and active play.

It is also vital to lead by example. When parents and caregivers actively participate in outdoor activities, children are more likely to follow suit. Setting aside time for family hikes, bike rides, or even backyard games can ignite a child's enthusiasm for the outdoors. Encouraging children to invite friends along can further enhance their social skills and create a sense of community. These shared experiences help children understand the value of play beyond screens and instill lifelong habits of physical activity.

Furthermore, creating an inviting outdoor space at home can significantly influence children's willingness to play outside. Simple additions like a sandbox, a small garden, or sports equipment can transform a backyard into an engaging playground. This not only provides a safe environment for children to play but also encourages imaginative play and exploration. Parents can involve children in the creation and maintenance of these spaces, fostering a sense of ownership and responsibility.

Lastly, balancing technology use with outdoor play requires intentionality and communication. Discussing the importance of outdoor activities with children can help them understand why it matters. Setting clear boundaries around screen time and encouraging self-regulation will enable children to make better choices about their activities. By fostering a culture of outdoor play, parents and caregivers can help children thrive in a tech-heavy world, ensuring they grow into well-rounded individuals who appreciate both the digital and natural realms.

# 4

# Educational Apps and Tools for Preschoolers

## Criteria for selecting educational apps

When selecting educational apps for young children, it is essential to prioritize content that aligns with their developmental stages and learning objectives. Start by evaluating the app's educational value. Look for applications that promote cognitive skills such as problem-solving, critical thinking, and creativity. Apps should also facilitate language development, offering rich vocabulary and opportunities for verbal interaction. A well-designed educational app not only entertains but also actively engages children in meaningful learning experiences that support their growth.

Another crucial criterion is the age appropriateness of the app. Verify that the app is tailored for your child's specific age group, as this ensures that the content is relatable and understandable. Apps meant for toddlers should focus on basic concepts like colors, shapes, and numbers, while preschoolers might benefit from activities that enhance literacy and social skills. Additionally, consider the user interface; it should be intuitive and easy for young children to navigate independently. This empowers them to explore and learn without constant adult supervision, fostering independence and self-confidence.

The design and interactivity of the app play a significant role in keeping children engaged. Look for apps that incorporate interactive elements such as touch, sound, and movement. These features can turn passive screen time into an active learning experience. Furthermore, apps that encourage hands-on activities or real-world connections can enhance the learning process. For example, an app that involves storytelling can prompt children to act out characters or create their own stories, bridging digital interaction with physical play.

Parental controls and monitoring features are also important factors when choosing educational apps. Opt for apps that allow you to set time limits, monitor usage, and customize content based on your family's values. This helps establish healthy boundaries around screen time and ensures that children are using technology in a constructive way. Additionally, consider apps that provide feedback or progress reports, enabling you to track your child's learning and engagement over time.

Lastly, seek out apps that encourage social interaction, either through cooperative play or by sharing achievements with others. Apps that allow children to collaborate on projects or compete in a friendly manner can enhance social skills and foster a sense of community. As you navigate the digital playground, remember that the goal is not just to entertain but to enrich your child's educational journey. By carefully selecting educational apps based on these criteria, you can create a balanced approach to technology that enhances learning while nurturing a love for exploration and discovery.

## Overview of popular educational tools

In today's digital landscape, a variety of educational tools are available that can significantly enhance children's learning experiences. These tools range from interactive apps and online games to educational websites and digital storytelling platforms. By leveraging technology, parents, teachers, and caregivers can create engaging and dynamic learning environments that cater to the unique needs and interests of young children. Understanding the options available is essential for making informed decisions about when and how to introduce these tools to children, ensuring that they contribute positively to their development.

One of the most popular categories of educational tools is mobile applications designed specifically for preschoolers. These apps often incorporate interactive elements, such as puzzles, quizzes, and storytelling, to keep young learners engaged. Many of these applications emphasize foundational skills, such as literacy and numeracy, while also encouraging creativity and critical thinking. As children interact with these tools, they can develop essential cognitive abilities while having fun. It is crucial for parents and caregivers to choose age-appropriate apps that align with their child's developmental stage, ensuring a balance between screen time and other activities.

Online platforms that offer educational games and activities have also gained popularity among young learners. Websites like ABCmouse and Starfall provide comprehensive learning experiences that cover various subjects, including math, reading, and science. These platforms often feature progress tracking, allowing parents and educators to monitor children's achievements and tailor learning paths to their needs. By selecting high-quality online resources, caregivers can foster a love of learning and support skill development in an engaging way, blending technology with traditional educational approaches.

Digital storytelling tools are another innovative technology that can enrich children's learning experiences. Platforms like Storybird and Toontastic allow children to create their own stories using images, animations, and sound. This not only enhances their creativity and self-expression but also helps develop literacy skills as they learn to structure narratives and convey ideas. Such tools can facilitate collaborative learning experiences when used in group settings, promoting communication and teamwork among peers. Parents can encourage storytelling by providing opportunities for children to share their creations with family members or friends.

While these educational tools offer numerous benefits, it is essential for parents and caregivers to establish boundaries and monitor technology use effectively. Setting guidelines for screen time, encouraging breaks for outdoor play, and integrating technology with family bonding activities can help ensure a balanced approach. By fostering open communication about technology and its role in children's lives, caregivers can help young learners navigate the digital world safely and responsibly. As technology continues to evolve, staying informed about the latest educational tools will empower parents and caregivers to make choices that support their children's growth and development.

## Integrating apps into learning routines

Integrating apps into learning routines can significantly enhance the educational experience for young children when done thoughtfully. At the heart of effective integration lies the understanding that technology should not replace traditional learning methods but rather complement them. Parents, babysitters, and educators can introduce educational apps as tools that reinforce concepts taught in the classroom or at home. The key is to select age-appropriate apps that align with the child's developmental stage, ensuring that the content is engaging and relevant. By participating in app usage together, caregivers can help children connect digital experiences with real-world applications, fostering a deeper understanding of the material.

Establishing a consistent routine for app usage is essential for maximizing their educational benefits. Setting aside specific times for app interaction can help children develop a balanced approach to technology use. For instance, caregivers might designate a "learning hour" where educational apps are used, followed by outdoor play or creative activities. This routine not only instills discipline but also encourages children to anticipate and look forward to their learning time. By integrating app usage into existing routines, such as incorporating educational games during snack time or using storytelling apps before bed, caregivers can seamlessly weave technology into daily life while maintaining a healthy balance with other activities.

When selecting apps, it's crucial to prioritize those that promote active engagement rather than passive consumption. Interactive apps that encourage problem-solving, critical thinking, and creativity can be especially beneficial. For example, apps that allow children to create stories, solve puzzles, or explore virtual environments can stimulate their imagination while aligning with educational goals. Additionally, many apps offer features that adapt to a child's learning pace, providing personalized experiences that can enhance their understanding and retention of information. Caregivers should familiarize themselves with the content and functionalities of each app to ensure that they are providing enriching experiences that support the child's growth.

Monitoring the use of technology is also a vital aspect of integrating apps into learning routines. Caregivers should take an active role in overseeing app interactions, discussing the content with children and encouraging them to articulate what they've learned. This dialogue not only reinforces comprehension but also promotes digital literacy, teaching children to navigate technology thoughtfully and responsibly. Setting boundaries around technology use, such as limiting screen time and ensuring that educational apps are utilized in moderation, can help prevent overreliance on digital tools and maintain a balanced lifestyle.

Finally, technology can serve as a powerful catalyst for family bonding. By engaging in app-based activities together, families can create shared experiences that strengthen relationships. Whether it's collaborating on a digital art project, solving a math game, or exploring a science app, these moments can spark conversations and foster teamwork. Integrating educational apps into family routines not only enhances learning but also transforms technology into a vehicle for connection. As caregivers embrace this integration with intention, they can cultivate an environment where technology enriches the learning experience while supporting overall child development.

# Technology in Early Childhood Education

## Benefits of technology in the classroom

The integration of technology in the classroom offers numerous benefits that can significantly enhance the learning experience for young children. One of the primary advantages is the accessibility of information. Digital tools provide students with a wealth of resources at their fingertips, allowing them to explore topics in depth and at their own pace. This access fosters a sense of independence and curiosity, encouraging children to ask questions and seek answers in ways that traditional textbooks may not facilitate. As parents and caregivers, recognizing this potential can guide us in choosing appropriate technological resources that align with our children's learning needs.

Technology also supports diverse learning styles and needs, making education more inclusive. Interactive software and educational apps can cater to visual, auditory, and kinesthetic learners alike. For instance, children who struggle with reading can benefit from audiobooks or interactive storytelling apps that make learning engaging. This adaptability not only helps to keep children motivated but also allows educators to tailor their teaching methods to accommodate the unique strengths and challenges of each student. By fostering an inclusive environment, technology contributes to a more equitable educational landscape.

Moreover, technology promotes collaboration and communication among students. Tools such as collaborative platforms and online discussion boards enable children to work together on projects, share ideas, and provide feedback to one another. This collaborative spirit is essential for developing social skills and teamwork, which are increasingly important in our interconnected world. Parents and caregivers can encourage children to engage in group activities that utilize technology, reinforcing the idea that learning is not just an individual pursuit but also a communal experience.

In addition, the use of technology in education can enhance critical thinking and problem-solving skills. Many educational games and apps challenge children to think critically and make decisions based on their actions. These activities encourage children to experiment, learn from mistakes, and develop resilience—a crucial aspect of their cognitive development. As caregivers, we can support this growth by introducing our children to technology that emphasizes these skills, ensuring they not only consume information but also engage with it thoughtfully.

Finally, integrating technology into the classroom can bolster family involvement in education. Many schools now utilize online portals where parents can track their child's progress, access resources, and communicate with teachers. This connectivity allows caregivers to stay informed and engaged in their child's learning journey, fostering a stronger partnership between home and school. By embracing technology in education, we can create a richer and more supportive learning environment for our children, paving the way for their future success in an increasingly digital world.

## Examples of tech integration in early education

In the landscape of early education, technology can play a transformative role when integrated thoughtfully. One prominent example is the use of interactive whiteboards in preschool classrooms. These boards facilitate dynamic lessons where children can engage directly with content. For instance, teachers can use them to display educational games that promote literacy and numeracy skills. During these sessions, children can participate in group activities, allowing them to develop social skills alongside their academic learning. This not only makes learning more engaging but also fosters collaboration and communication among young learners.

Another effective integration of technology is through the use of tablets equipped with educational apps. For toddlers and preschoolers, there are numerous applications designed specifically for their developmental stage. These apps often incorporate playful elements that encourage creativity and critical thinking. For example, drawing apps allow children to express their artistic abilities while learning about colors and shapes. When parents or caregivers guide children in using these tools, they can create a rich learning environment that balances screen time with meaningful interactions, reinforcing concepts through discussion and shared experiences.

Additionally, technology can enhance outdoor play experiences. Wearable devices, such as fitness trackers, can be introduced to encourage physical activity in a fun way. Children can set simple goals, track their steps, and even earn rewards for reaching milestones. This integration not only promotes a healthy lifestyle but also helps children understand the importance of physical activity through technology. Parents can facilitate this by organizing outdoor playdates where technology is used to enhance the experience, ensuring that children remain active while also learning about goal-setting and achievement.

Storytelling applications are another valuable tool in early education. These apps often allow children to create their own stories by combining images, text, and audio. By using storytelling apps, children can develop literacy skills while also learning how to express themselves creatively. When parents take part in this process, it becomes a bonding activity that encourages dialogue and imagination. This collaborative storytelling not only enhances language development but also fosters a love for reading and narrative comprehension early on.

Finally, technology can serve as a bridge for family bonding activities. Video calls and interactive games allow families to connect with distant relatives or friends, creating shared experiences that enhance emotional bonds. For example, grandparents can read stories to their grandchildren via video chat, making use of technology to maintain relationships despite physical distance. Parents can also set aside time for family game nights using online platforms that promote teamwork and problem-solving skills. By integrating technology in these ways, families not only enjoy quality time together but also model healthy technology use for their children, setting the stage for balanced habits as they grow.

## Professional development for educators

Professional development for educators is crucial in equipping them with the knowledge and skills needed to effectively integrate technology into early childhood education. As technology continues to evolve, it is essential for teachers and childcare providers to stay abreast of the latest tools, trends, and methodologies. This ongoing education helps ensure that they can provide age-appropriate technology experiences that enrich learning while fostering a healthy balance between screen time and outdoor activities.

Workshops and training programs focused on technology use in the classroom can empower educators to confidently introduce digital tools in meaningful ways. These professional development opportunities often cover topics such as selecting educational apps that promote cognitive and social skills, as well as understanding the developmental appropriateness of various technologies. By participating in these sessions, educators can share best practices and learn from their peers, ultimately enhancing their collective ability to guide young children in their technology use.

Collaboration among educators is another vital aspect of professional development. Establishing a network or community of practice allows teachers to discuss challenges and successes in implementing technology in their classrooms. This exchange of ideas fosters innovation and encourages the development of strategies that are both effective and respectful of children's developmental needs. When educators work together, they can create a more supportive environment for children navigating the digital landscape.

Furthermore, professional development should also include training on digital literacy and responsible technology use. Educators play a key role in teaching young children how to navigate online environments safely and ethically. By fostering digital literacy from an early age, teachers can help children develop critical thinking skills that are necessary in today's technology-driven world. This foundation prepares children for future academic challenges and promotes responsible behavior as they grow older.

Finally, ongoing professional development for educators serves as a model for parents and caregivers. When educators are well-informed and proactive about technology integration, they can share valuable insights with families. This collaboration encourages a consistent approach to technology use at home and in educational settings, ensuring that children receive a cohesive message about engaging with digital tools. As parents and caregivers witness their children's positive experiences with technology guided by knowledgeable educators, they are more likely to embrace and support these practices within their own families.

# 6

# Setting Boundaries for Technology Use in School

## Establishing family tech rules

Establishing family tech rules is a crucial step in ensuring that technology serves as a beneficial tool rather than a disruptive force in your household. One of the first steps is to engage your children in the conversation about technology use. Discussing the reasons behind the rules fosters a sense of ownership and responsibility. By including them in the rule-making process, you not only empower them but also encourage them to think critically about their own tech habits. This collaborative approach promotes a healthier relationship with technology, allowing children to feel heard and understood.

When creating these rules, it's important to consider age-appropriate guidelines tailored to your child's developmental stage. For toddlers, the focus should be on limited screen time and ensuring that technology is used primarily for educational purposes, such as interactive storybooks or learning apps. As children grow, rules can evolve to include more complex technologies while still emphasizing the importance of balance. For elementary-aged children, integrating tech use with outdoor play is essential. Setting specific timeframes for tech use helps children learn to manage their time effectively, allowing for both screen time and physical activity.

Monitoring technology use is another vital component of establishing effective family tech rules. Parents and caregivers should regularly check in on what children are engaging with online, ensuring that content is appropriate and educational. Creating a family media plan can be a helpful tool in this regard, outlining what types of technology are acceptable, when they can be used, and which apps or websites are suitable. Regular discussions about the content children are consuming can enhance their digital literacy, helping them understand the difference between constructive and harmful media.

As children transition into the tween years, the conversation around social media exposure becomes increasingly important. Setting clear guidelines about social media usage can protect children from potential pitfalls while still allowing them to connect with peers. Encourage open dialogue about their online experiences, teaching them about privacy settings and the importance of maintaining a positive digital footprint. This approach not only safeguards their online presence but also fosters trust between parents and children, making them more likely to share their online experiences and concerns.

Lastly, technology can serve as a powerful tool for family bonding when used wisely. Establishing tech rules that promote shared experiences, such as family game nights or group educational activities, can enhance relationships while reinforcing the value of technology in a positive light. By making tech use a collective experience, families can navigate the digital playground together, creating lasting memories and meaningful connections. Balancing structured rules with opportunities for fun can help families thrive in this digital age, ensuring that technology enriches rather than detracts from their time together.

## The importance of consistency

Consistency plays a pivotal role in navigating the digital landscape with young children. Establishing clear and predictable guidelines around technology use helps children understand expectations and develop healthy relationships with their devices. When parents, babysitters, teachers, and childcare givers consistently apply rules regarding screen time, children are more likely to adapt to these boundaries. This predictability fosters a sense of security, enabling children to thrive in their explorations of technology while feeling supported by the adults in their lives.

Incorporating consistency into technology use also aids in balancing screen time with outdoor play and other activities. When caregivers set a standard routine that allocates specific times for technology and encourages outdoor play, children learn to appreciate both digital and physical experiences. For instance, designating certain hours for educational apps after outdoor play not only reinforces the importance of varied activities but also nurtures a well-rounded development. This approach helps children develop an understanding of time management, as they learn to navigate their interests within structured limits.

Furthermore, consistent messaging about age-appropriate technology use is essential for fostering digital literacy in young children. By repeatedly discussing what constitutes safe and suitable content, caregivers empower children to make informed choices as they interact with technology. This ongoing dialogue encourages critical thinking and helps children discern between different types of media, ultimately enhancing their ability to engage thoughtfully with technology. Emphasizing these values consistently lays the groundwork for responsible technology use as children grow older.

As children progress into elementary school, maintaining consistent boundaries around technology becomes even more crucial. It is vital for caregivers to adapt their guidelines as children encounter new digital experiences, such as social media and online games. By reinforcing rules and expectations, caregivers can help children navigate potential pitfalls associated with increased technology exposure. This consistency aids in building resilience, as children learn to recognize and manage distractions while developing their social skills in both digital and real-life contexts.

Finally, consistency in technology use can also strengthen family bonds. When families engage in shared digital experiences, such as playing educational games together or watching age-appropriate shows, they create opportunities for connection and communication. Establishing regular family tech time fosters discussions about digital content and its implications, reinforcing the importance of shared values in a tech-rich environment. By being consistent in their approach to technology, caregivers not only guide children in their digital exploration but also enrich family relationships through collaborative experiences.

## Encouraging responsible technology use

Encouraging responsible technology use begins with understanding the developmental stages of children and the role technology plays in their lives. As parents and caregivers, it is essential to introduce technology in a way that complements their growth rather than detracts from it. By framing technology as a tool for learning and creativity, we can nurture a balanced approach that fosters curiosity, enhances educational experiences, and encourages social interaction. Establishing clear guidelines on when and how technology should be introduced allows for a smoother transition into the digital world while ensuring that children remain engaged with their surroundings.

Age-appropriate technology use is crucial for toddlers and preschoolers. At this stage, children are naturally inclined to explore their environment, and technology can serve as an extension of that curiosity. Selecting educational apps that promote problem-solving skills, creativity, and basic literacy can enhance their learning experience. However, it's important to limit screen time and focus on interactive, high-quality content. This not only helps children absorb information but also provides opportunities for parents and caregivers to engage alongside them, creating shared moments that strengthen relationships.

Balancing screen time with outdoor play is another significant aspect of responsible technology use. While digital tools can be beneficial, excessive screen time can lead to sedentary lifestyles, impacting physical health and social skills. Encouraging children to spend time outdoors, engage in physical activities, and interact with peers helps them develop essential skills and resilience. Setting aside specific times for technology use, combined with outdoor play and creative activities, establishes a well-rounded routine that fosters health and well-being.

As children progress into elementary school, it becomes vital to set boundaries for technology use. Families can create a technology plan that includes designated screen time limits, guidelines for content consumption, and opportunities for offline activities. This approach not only helps monitor usage but also encourages children to take responsibility for their choices. Teaching digital literacy skills, including understanding online safety and recognizing credible sources, empowers kids to navigate the digital landscape confidently and responsibly.

Finally, technology can also play a role in family bonding activities. Engaging in shared technology experiences, such as playing educational games, watching documentaries, or creating digital art together, can strengthen family ties while providing platforms for discussion and learning. By modeling responsible technology use and demonstrating its potential for positive interaction, parents and caregivers can instill values of respect, empathy, and critical thinking in their children. This holistic approach to technology not only prepares children for the future but also ensures they develop a healthy relationship with it throughout their lives.

7

# The Impact of Technology on Child Development

## Cognitive development and technology

Cognitive development in early childhood is a multifaceted process that can be influenced by various factors, including technology. As parents, babysitters, teachers, and childcare givers, understanding the interplay between technology and cognitive growth is essential. When introduced appropriately, technology can enhance learning experiences, stimulate curiosity, and promote problem-solving skills. The key is to recognize that not all technology is created equal; age-appropriate content and applications can support developmental milestones while ensuring that children remain engaged and active participants in their learning journey.

For toddlers, the introduction of technology should be approached with caution. At this stage, children benefit most from interactive and hands-on experiences that foster exploration and creativity. While certain educational apps designed for young children can encourage cognitive skills through playful interaction, it is vital to limit screen time to ensure that these digital experiences do not replace essential outdoor play and social interactions. Balancing screen time with physical activities not only supports physical health but also enhances cognitive skills through real-world exploration and engagement with peers.

As children transition to preschool and early elementary school, educational apps and tools can play a significant role in their cognitive development. High-quality educational resources can provide personalized learning experiences that cater to individual needs, helping children develop foundational skills in literacy, numeracy, and critical thinking. These tools can complement traditional learning methods and offer opportunities for children to explore concepts at their own pace. However, parents and caregivers should remain vigilant in selecting appropriate content that aligns with developmental goals, ensuring that technology serves as a beneficial supplement rather than a distraction.

Setting boundaries for technology use becomes increasingly important as children grow older and are exposed to a wider array of digital content. Establishing clear guidelines about when and how technology can be used not only helps children develop self-regulation skills but also fosters a healthy relationship with devices. Engaging children in discussions about screen time and encouraging them to reflect on their experiences with technology can empower them to make informed choices. Additionally, creating technology-free zones and times, such as during meals or family activities, promotes meaningful interactions and strengthens family bonds.

Finally, teaching digital literacy to young children is crucial for preparing them to navigate the increasingly digital world. Understanding how to use technology responsibly, recognizing online safety, and being aware of the implications of social media are essential skills for today's youth. Parents and caregivers can model positive technology use and engage children in conversations about their online experiences. By incorporating technology into family bonding activities and encouraging collaborative play with digital tools, caregivers can ensure that children develop not only cognitive skills but also the social and emotional competencies needed to thrive in a technology-rich environment.

## Social and emotional effects

The integration of technology into the lives of young children can profoundly influence their social and emotional development. As parents and caregivers, it is essential to recognize that the digital landscape offers both opportunities and challenges for fostering healthy social interactions. Young children, still in the formative stages of developing emotional intelligence and interpersonal skills, may find themselves navigating a complex world where face-to-face interactions compete with virtual connections. Understanding these dynamics will help caregivers create a balanced environment that promotes healthy relationships.

One significant effect of technology on young children is the potential for reduced face-to-face social interactions. When children engage with screens for extended periods, they may miss out on critical opportunities to develop social skills, such as sharing, cooperation, and empathy. This can lead to difficulties in understanding social cues and managing emotions. Encouraging outdoor play and group activities can counteract this trend. By providing opportunities for children to interact with peers in person, caregivers can help cultivate essential social skills and emotional resilience.

Moreover, the emotional responses elicited by technology can vary significantly based on the content consumed. Educational apps and games can foster a sense of achievement and boost self-esteem, while exposure to inappropriate content or excessive social media can lead to anxiety and feelings of inadequacy. Parents and caregivers should carefully curate the types of technology their children engage with, ensuring that they are age-appropriate and promote positive emotional responses. This intentional approach can empower children to use technology as a tool for growth rather than a source of distress.

In addition to content, the context in which technology is used plays a crucial role in shaping its social and emotional effects. Family bonding activities that incorporate technology, such as interactive games or educational apps, can strengthen relationships and create shared experiences. These moments not only provide valuable learning opportunities but also foster emotional connections between family members. By modeling healthy technology use, caregivers can demonstrate that technology can enhance rather than hinder relationships.

Ultimately, the goal is to cultivate a balanced approach to technology that supports social and emotional development. Setting clear boundaries around screen time and encouraging a diverse range of activities—both digital and physical—will help children thrive in an increasingly digital world. By prioritizing meaningful interactions and providing guidance on responsible technology use, parents and caregivers can equip young children with the skills they need to navigate the complexities of their digital playground while fostering their emotional well-being.

## Long-term implications for technology use

The long-term implications of technology use in early childhood are significant and multifaceted, shaping not only the immediate experiences of young children but also their future development and interactions with the world. As parents and caregivers introduce technology to toddlers and preschoolers, it becomes essential to consider how these early encounters may influence cognitive, social, and emotional growth. By understanding these implications, caregivers can create a balanced approach that promotes healthy technology usage while fostering essential developmental skills.

One major implication of technology use is the potential impact on cognitive development. Engaging with age-appropriate educational apps and tools can enhance learning experiences by introducing interactive elements that stimulate curiosity and critical thinking. However, it's equally important to ensure that screen time is complemented with hands-on activities. This balance helps children develop problem-solving skills, creativity, and fine motor skills, essential for their overall intellectual growth. By curating a mix of digital and physical play, caregivers can nurture a well-rounded developmental environment.

Social interactions are another crucial area affected by technology. While digital platforms can facilitate connections with family and friends, excessive screen time may hinder the development of face-to-face communication skills. Encouraging outdoor play and interpersonal activities can help children learn vital social cues, empathy, and teamwork. Establishing boundaries around technology use, particularly during formative years, can promote healthier social habits and ensure that children engage in meaningful interactions beyond the screen.

Moreover, the role of technology in early childhood education cannot be overlooked. When used effectively, technology can enhance learning opportunities, providing access to diverse resources and information. Educational tools can support individualized learning paths, catering to varying developmental stages and learning styles. However, caregivers must remain vigilant in selecting high-quality content and fostering a critical approach to technology. Teaching digital literacy from a young age prepares children to navigate the digital landscape responsibly, equipping them with skills to discern credible information and engage positively online.

Finally, the long-term implications of technology use extend to family dynamics as well. Technology can serve as a bonding tool, enabling families to share experiences through games, videos, and collaborative projects. Establishing tech-free zones or times can enhance family interactions and encourage open communication. By fostering a healthy technology culture within the home, caregivers can model positive behaviors and set expectations that promote balanced lifestyles. Ultimately, the goal is to equip children with the tools they need to thrive in a digital world while ensuring they remain connected to the joys of life beyond the screen.

# 8

# Teaching Digital Literacy to Young Children

## What is digital literacy?

Digital literacy encompasses a range of skills that allow individuals to navigate, evaluate, and create information using digital technologies. For young children, this foundational ability is crucial as they begin to interact with screens and devices. Digital literacy is not merely about being able to use technology; it also involves understanding how to use it responsibly and effectively. This knowledge empowers children to engage with digital content critically and creatively, providing them with the tools they need to thrive in an increasingly tech-driven world.

Introducing digital literacy to young children can start as early as preschool. At this stage, children can learn basic skills such as identifying different devices, understanding how to use touchscreens, and recognizing simple icons. Age-appropriate technology use for toddlers can include educational apps that promote learning through play. These tools can help develop fine motor skills and cognitive abilities while teaching children how to interact with technology in a safe and engaging manner. As parents, babysitters, and educators, it is important to select applications and tools that are designed with young users in mind, ensuring that they are both educational and enjoyable.

Balancing screen time with outdoor play is essential for healthy development. Digital literacy is not just about the time spent on devices; it also involves teaching children the importance of offline activities. Encouraging physical play, creativity, and social interactions away from screens fosters a well-rounded skill set. Parents can model this balance by setting limits on screen time while also participating in outdoor activities or creative projects with their children. This approach helps instill a sense of moderation and teaches children that while technology can be a valuable resource, it is equally important to engage with the world around them.

As children progress into elementary school, digital literacy continues to evolve. This stage often involves the introduction of more complex technology and the internet. Teaching children about online safety, privacy, and respectful communication is vital. Setting boundaries for technology use in this age group helps children understand the importance of responsible digital citizenship. Parents can implement family rules regarding technology use, such as designated tech-free times or areas in the home, promoting a healthy balance between digital engagement and family bonding activities.

Ultimately, the goal of fostering digital literacy in young children is to equip them with skills that will serve them throughout their lives. By teaching them how to evaluate information critically, engage positively in online communities, and create their own digital content, we prepare them for future success. The role of technology in early childhood education is significant, and when approached thoughtfully, it can enhance learning experiences while nurturing essential life skills. Through active involvement and guidance, parents, teachers, and caregivers can help children become not only proficient users of technology but also informed and responsible digital citizens.

## Age-appropriate strategies for teaching

Age-appropriate strategies for teaching technology to young children begin with understanding their developmental stages and recognizing that each age group has unique needs and capabilities. For toddlers, introducing technology should be done with care, focusing on interactive and engaging tools that promote exploration rather than passive consumption. Simple touchscreen devices that offer educational games can be beneficial, but parents and caregivers should prioritize hands-on activities that foster creativity and physical coordination. Incorporating technology into playtime can enhance learning, but it is essential to balance this with traditional play that encourages social interaction and problem-solving skills.

As children transition to preschool age, the focus can shift toward educational apps and tools designed to support early literacy and numeracy skills. At this stage, parents and caregivers can introduce technology that complements their learning experiences, such as interactive storybooks or games that encourage counting and letter recognition. It's vital to establish a routine that includes these tools while also emphasizing the importance of outdoor play and physical activity. Research shows that children who engage in a mix of screen time and outdoor play develop better social skills and cognitive abilities.

In elementary school, children are often ready for more structured technology use, including learning about digital literacy and online safety. Parents can guide their children in navigating the digital world by setting clear boundaries around technology use. This includes defining times for using devices, encouraging breaks, and promoting a healthy balance between screen time and other activities. Engaging children in discussions about what they encounter online can help them develop critical thinking skills and a sense of responsibility regarding their digital footprint.

Teaching digital literacy becomes increasingly important as children grow older and start using social media. Parents and caregivers should provide age-appropriate lessons on privacy, sharing information responsibly, and understanding the implications of their online actions. Creating a family media plan can help outline expectations and promote safe technology use. Encouraging children to express their thoughts on the content they see online can foster open communication and critical analysis, which are essential skills in today's digital landscape.

Finally, technology can play a significant role in family bonding activities. Parents can leverage devices to create shared experiences, such as watching educational shows together, playing interactive games, or exploring virtual museums. Such activities can foster connection while also teaching children how to use technology mindfully. By implementing these age-appropriate strategies, families can navigate the digital playground effectively, ensuring that technology enhances rather than detracts from children's developmental journeys.

## Resources for parents and educators

In the journey of introducing technology to young children, it is vital for parents and educators to have access to a wide range of resources that can guide their decisions and actions. Various organizations offer valuable insights and tools, including websites dedicated to child development and technology use. For example, the American Academy of Pediatrics provides guidelines on screen time for different age groups, emphasizing the importance of balancing technology with physical activity and interpersonal interactions. Parents can also explore the Zero to Three organization, which focuses on early childhood development and offers practical tips for integrating technology in a healthy manner.

Educational apps and software can be another great resource for parents and educators. Platforms like Common Sense Media provide detailed reviews of apps and games that are age-appropriate and educational. These reviews consider factors such as content quality, educational value, and developmental appropriateness, helping caregivers make informed choices. Additionally, many libraries and community centers offer free access to educational resources, including interactive learning tools that can engage young minds in a screen-safe environment. Utilizing these community resources not only enhances learning but also fosters a sense of belonging and connection.

To address the challenges of balancing screen time with outdoor play, families can refer to various guides and articles that offer practical strategies. Organizations such as the National Wildlife Federation promote outdoor play as essential for healthy development and provide resources for creating tech-free zones. Parents can implement family rules that designate specific times for technology use while encouraging outdoor activities, thus teaching children the value of a balanced lifestyle. Resources like parenting blogs and forums can also offer ideas for outdoor activities that incorporate learning and exploration, making the most of children's time outside.

Teaching digital literacy is crucial in today's technology-driven world. Programs like Google's Be Internet Awesome provide engaging lessons on online safety, privacy, and digital citizenship, tailored specifically for young learners. Parents and educators can implement these lessons in their routines, creating opportunities for discussions about responsible technology use. Additionally, local schools often host workshops or seminars on digital literacy, equipping caregivers with the knowledge to guide their children as they navigate the digital landscape.

Lastly, reinforcing family bonding through technology can be achieved by utilizing available resources that promote shared experiences. Websites like Family Education offer suggestions for tech-based family activities, such as coding games or interactive storytelling apps, that can be enjoyed together. These activities not only foster a strong family connection but also create a collaborative environment where children can learn from their parents. By prioritizing shared technology use and setting clear boundaries, parents and educators can ensure that technology serves as a tool for growth, learning, and enhancing relationships within the family.

# 9

# Strategies for Parents to Monitor Technology Use

## Tools and applications for monitoring

In the evolving landscape of technology, monitoring tools and applications have become essential for parents, babysitters, teachers, and childcare givers who wish to navigate the digital playground with young children. These tools not only provide insights into how children engage with technology but also help establish boundaries that promote healthy technology use. By utilizing these resources, caregivers can ensure that children's interactions with devices are age-appropriate and aligned with their developmental needs.

One of the most effective categories of monitoring tools is parental control applications. These applications allow caregivers to track screen time, set usage limits, and filter content to ensure that children are accessing appropriate materials. Popular options such as Qustodio, Norton Family, and Bark offer comprehensive features that enable caregivers to monitor app usage, block inappropriate websites, and receive alerts about potential risks. By using these tools, caregivers can maintain a balance between allowing children the freedom to explore technology and protecting them from harmful content.

In addition to parental control applications, educational tools can play a significant role in monitoring technology use. Many educational apps designed for preschoolers and toddlers come with built-in analytics that track progress and engagement. Platforms like ABCmouse and Starfall provide insights into a child's learning journey, allowing caregivers to assess which areas need more attention and which apps are most beneficial. This data can guide parents in selecting age-appropriate technology that fosters learning while ensuring that screen time is productive and educational.

Balancing screen time with outdoor play is another critical aspect of monitoring technology use. Applications that promote physical activity, such as GoNoodle and Sworkit Kids, can help caregivers encourage children to engage in active play while still incorporating technology. These tools allow caregivers to set reminders for physical activity breaks and track the amount of time children spend on screens versus outdoors. By fostering a balanced approach, caregivers can ensure that technology complements rather than replaces physical activity, contributing to a healthier lifestyle for young children.

Finally, teaching digital literacy is an essential component of monitoring technology use in early childhood education. Resources that promote safe online practices and responsible use of technology can empower children to make informed choices as they engage with digital content. Programs that involve interactive lessons on internet safety, privacy, and digital citizenship can help instill a sense of responsibility in young users. By introducing these concepts early on, caregivers can create a foundation for healthy technology habits that will support children as they grow and encounter more complex digital environments.

## Setting up tech-free zones

Creating tech-free zones in your home or classroom can significantly enhance the quality of interaction among children and help them develop essential social skills. These designated areas, free from screens and digital distractions, encourage face-to-face communication, imaginative play, and a deeper connection with the physical world. To establish such zones effectively, it's important to choose specific locations within your home or childcare setting where technology is not allowed. Common choices include dining areas, playrooms, or even outdoor spaces where children can engage in various activities without the interference of devices.

To ensure that these tech-free zones are engaging and appealing to young children, consider incorporating a variety of activities that stimulate their creativity and curiosity. Board games, art supplies, building blocks, and books can all be excellent additions to these spaces. By providing a range of options, you invite children to explore different forms of play and learning, fostering their imagination and problem-solving skills. Regularly rotating these activities can keep the environment fresh and exciting, encouraging children to return to these zones time and again.

Establishing rules and expectations for tech-free zones helps reinforce the importance of these spaces. Communicate clearly with children about the purpose of these areas, emphasizing that they are meant for social interaction, creativity, and relaxation. Setting specific times when these zones are in use can further reinforce their significance. For instance, family meals could be a designated tech-free time where everyone engages in conversation and connection without digital interruptions, promoting healthier relationships and communication skills.

Involving children in the creation and maintenance of these zones can increase their investment in the process. Encourage them to choose which activities or games they would like to include, allowing them to take ownership of their tech-free environment. This collaboration not only makes children more likely to engage in these zones but also teaches them valuable lessons about teamwork and decision-making. Furthermore, it opens up discussions about the benefits of balancing technology with other forms of play and learning.

Lastly, it's essential to model the behavior you wish to see in children. Adults should also participate in tech-free time, demonstrating the enjoyment and fulfillment that can come from engaging with one another without screens. By doing so, you reinforce the importance of these zones and provide a positive example for children to emulate. As they observe adults valuing real-life interactions over digital distractions, they are more likely to internalize these lessons, laying the groundwork for healthier technology habits as they grow.

### Engaging in conversations about tech use

Engaging in conversations about tech use with young children is essential for fostering a healthy relationship between kids and technology. Parents, caregivers, and educators play a critical role in guiding children through their early interactions with digital devices. By initiating open dialogues about technology, adults can help children understand its benefits and challenges, making them more informed users. These conversations can start as early as toddlerhood, focusing on the types of technology that are age-appropriate and encouraging curiosity, creativity, and learning.

When discussing technology with toddlers, it is important to select tools that promote interactive play rather than passive consumption. Engaging with educational apps designed for this age group can provide a fun way to introduce basic concepts like shapes, colors, and numbers. Parents should express enthusiasm about exploring these tools together, reinforcing that technology is a means of learning and connecting rather than a distraction. This collaborative approach not only enhances the child's understanding but also strengthens the bond between the adult and the child.

As children grow and begin to navigate the digital landscape more independently, establishing boundaries becomes crucial. Open discussions about screen time can help children understand the importance of balancing technology use with outdoor play and other activities. It's beneficial to set specific times for screen use and encourage children to participate in physical activities or creative play during non-screen hours. Such conversations can help children develop essential skills in time management and self-regulation, which are vital as they move into elementary school and beyond.

Incorporating conversations about technology into family activities can also deepen relationships and create shared experiences. Parents can invite children to suggest educational apps or games they enjoy, facilitating discussions about what they learn from these resources. This practice not only enhances children's engagement with technology but also teaches them to critically evaluate its content. By making tech use a family affair, parents can model positive behavior and establish a culture of responsible digital citizenship within the home.

Finally, teaching digital literacy should be an ongoing conversation as children grow. This includes discussing the impact of social media exposure, online safety, and digital footprints. Parents and caregivers can foster an environment where children feel comfortable asking questions about their online experiences. By maintaining an open dialogue, adults can reinforce their role as trusted advisors in navigating technology, ultimately empowering children to become confident, responsible users of digital tools as they mature.

# 10

# Social Media Exposure for Tweens

## Understanding the tween social media landscape

Understanding the tween social media landscape is essential for parents, caregivers, and educators as children begin to explore their identities and friendships online. At this age, tweens are typically between the ages of 9 and 12, a critical developmental stage where they seek independence and social acceptance. Social media platforms provide a space for self-expression and connection, but they also present unique challenges and risks. Familiarizing yourself with the various platforms that tweens gravitate towards can help you guide them in making informed choices about their online presence.

Popular social media sites among tweens include Instagram, TikTok, and Snapchat. Each platform offers different features that appeal to this age group, such as photo sharing, short videos, and ephemeral messaging. Understanding how these platforms work and what they promote is crucial for parents. For instance, TikTok emphasizes creativity and entertainment, but it also exposes users to trends that may not always align with family values. By engaging in conversations about the content they encounter, parents can help tweens navigate these spaces more safely.

Moreover, the tween social media landscape is heavily influenced by peer interactions. As children begin to form deeper friendships, they often turn to social media to maintain connections. This reliance on online communication can lead to both positive experiences, like developing social skills, and negative ones, such as cyberbullying or social anxiety. Parents and caregivers should encourage open discussions about online friendships and the emotions that arise from social media interactions. This dialogue can empower tweens to express their feelings and seek support when they encounter difficulties.

Setting healthy boundaries around social media use is vital for maintaining a balanced lifestyle. Parents can establish guidelines regarding screen time, the types of content allowed, and the amount of privacy tweens should have. These boundaries should be age-appropriate, ensuring that children feel both safe and independent. Encouraging regular breaks from screens and promoting outdoor activities can help maintain this balance, allowing tweens to enjoy both their online and offline worlds.

Finally, teaching digital literacy is an essential component in helping tweens navigate the social media landscape. This includes understanding the importance of privacy settings, recognizing misinformation, and developing critical thinking skills regarding online content. Parents can introduce these concepts through discussions, workshops, or even by modeling responsible online behavior themselves. By fostering a sense of digital responsibility, caregivers can help tweens build a healthy relationship with technology that supports their overall development.

## Guidelines for safe social media use

When guiding young children in their digital experiences, it is essential to establish clear guidelines for safe social media use. Parents, babysitters, teachers, and childcare givers should emphasize the importance of understanding privacy settings and the implications of sharing personal information online. Educating children about the potential risks associated with oversharing can empower them to make informed decisions about what to post, ensuring that their online presence remains secure. Encourage conversations about the types of information that are safe to share and those that should remain private, fostering a sense of responsibility in their digital interactions.

Monitoring the types of social media platforms children are using is another vital aspect of ensuring their safety. Parents and caregivers should familiarize themselves with the various platforms available and the specific features that cater to different age groups. This knowledge will help adults guide children toward age-appropriate social media experiences. Setting limits on the types of interactions children can have on these platforms, such as only allowing communication with known friends and family, can further protect them from unwanted encounters and harmful content.

Establishing a routine around social media use can also contribute significantly to a child's overall well-being. It is crucial to balance screen time with other activities, including outdoor play and family bonding exercises. Creating designated times for social media usage can help children understand that while technology can be enjoyable, it should not replace essential real-world experiences. Encouraging participation in physical activities and family outings can promote a healthy lifestyle while reinforcing the notion that social interactions can occur both online and offline.

Digital literacy is a key component in teaching young children to navigate social media safely. Parents and educators should introduce lessons about recognizing misinformation, understanding the permanence of online content, and the consequences of their online behavior. Teaching children how to critically evaluate the information they encounter, as well as how to respond to negative interactions or cyberbullying, will equip them with essential skills for their digital lives. This education should be an ongoing process, adapting as children grow and their social media interactions evolve.

Lastly, open communication about social media experiences is vital for fostering a safe digital environment. Encourage children to share their online activities and experiences without fear of judgment. Creating a space where they feel comfortable discussing their thoughts and concerns will help adults identify any potential issues early on. By fostering trust and maintaining an open dialogue, parents and caregivers can guide children through the complexities of social media while ensuring their safety and promoting healthy digital habits.

## Encouraging positive online interactions

Encouraging positive online interactions is essential in fostering a healthy relationship between children and technology. As parents, babysitters, teachers, and caregivers, it is crucial to model and promote respectful and constructive behaviors in digital spaces. By actively guiding children on how to communicate effectively and positively online, we can help them navigate the complexities of digital interactions while building their emotional intelligence and social skills. Establishing a foundation of kindness and respect in their online presence will serve them well as they grow and engage with diverse communities.

One effective approach to encourage positive online interactions is through open discussions about emotions and empathy. Engaging young children in conversations about how their words and actions can affect others lays the groundwork for thoughtful communication. Sharing stories or examples of positive and negative online interactions can help children understand the impact of their behavior. This dialogue not only raises awareness but also empowers them to make mindful choices when interacting with peers in digital environments, promoting a culture of kindness.

Moreover, introducing children to age-appropriate technology that emphasizes collaboration and constructive engagement can significantly enhance their online experiences. Educational apps and games that require teamwork or problem-solving encourage children to work together and communicate effectively. These platforms serve as practical tools to practice positive interactions, allowing children to experience firsthand the benefits of cooperation and mutual respect. By selecting technology that reinforces these values, caregivers can create an enriching digital landscape for young learners.

Setting clear boundaries regarding technology use is another vital aspect of encouraging positive online interactions. Establishing guidelines around screen time, content consumption, and the types of interactions allowed can help children feel secure and understand the importance of maintaining respectful behavior online. Families can collaboratively create a technology use agreement, outlining expectations and consequences, which not only fosters accountability but also encourages children to take ownership of their online actions. This structured approach helps cultivate a sense of responsibility and respect in their digital endeavors.

Finally, regular check-ins and open communication regarding children's online experiences can significantly enhance their ability to engage positively in digital spaces. By creating an environment where children feel comfortable discussing their online interactions, caregivers can provide guidance, support, and constructive feedback. This ongoing dialogue not only helps children navigate challenges they may face online but also reinforces the importance of kindness and empathy in all interactions. By encouraging positive online behaviors, we can equip the next generation with the skills they need to thrive in an increasingly digital world.

# 11

# The Role of Technology in Family Bonding Activity

## Ideas for tech-based family activities

In today's fast-paced digital world, finding ways to engage the entire family through technology can foster both learning and bonding. Tech-based family activities provide an opportunity to not only enjoy quality time together but also to educate and inspire creativity. Parents and caregivers can harness the power of technology to create enriching experiences that strengthen family ties while ensuring age-appropriate use. From interactive games to collaborative projects, the possibilities for tech-based family activities are vast and varied, making them an excellent addition to family routines.

One popular idea is to organize family game nights using educational apps or online games that promote teamwork and critical thinking. These games can be tailored to different age groups, ensuring that everyone can participate and contribute. For instance, younger children can engage with apps that enhance their problem-solving skills through fun puzzles, while older siblings might enjoy strategy games that require collaboration and planning. This not only fosters family bonding but also encourages children to develop essential cognitive skills in a supportive environment.

Another engaging activity is to create a family project using technology. This could involve making a digital scrapbook or video montage that highlights family memories, trips, or special events. Children can take ownership of the project by researching and selecting photos, writing captions, and learning basic video editing techniques. This hands-on experience promotes digital literacy and creativity, enabling children to express themselves

while learning valuable skills in a fun and meaningful way. Parents can guide them through the
process, providing support and encouragement as
they explore their artistic side.

Exploring the world through virtual field trips
is another fantastic tech-based family activity.
Many museums, zoos, and cultural institutions offer online tours that allow families to explore diverse environments from the comfort of their
home. This not only expands children's horizons
but also sparks curiosity about different cultures
and subjects. After the virtual visit, families can
discuss what they learned, fostering communication and critical thinking. This activity can also
serve as a springboard for further exploration, encouraging families to seek out related books, documentaries, or even in-person visits when possible.

Finally, families can engage in coding and ro-
botics activities that promote collaboration and
learning. Many age-appropriate coding platforms
and kits are designed for young children, making it
easy for families to work together to build simple
programs or robots. This hands-on experience in-
troduces basic programming concepts while em-

phasizing teamwork, as family members can contribute their unique skills and ideas. By participating in these activities, children gain confidence in their abilities and develop a foundation for understanding technology that will serve them well in the future.

Incorporating tech-based family activities into daily life not only enhances family bonding but also supports children's development in a balanced manner. By selecting age-appropriate tools and engaging in activities that promote learning and creativity, parents and caregivers can ensure that technology becomes a positive force in their children's lives. Emphasizing collaboration and open communication around these activities will help families navigate the digital playground together, fostering a healthy relationship with technology that promotes growth and connection.

## Balancing tech and traditional bonding experiences

In today's rapidly evolving digital landscape, finding a balance between technology and traditional bonding experiences is essential for fostering healthy relationships and development in young children. As parents, babysitters, teachers, and childcare givers, it is crucial to recognize that while technology offers valuable tools for learning and engagement, it should not overshadow the importance of face-to-face interactions and physical activities. By integrating both aspects into children's lives, we can create a rich environment that supports their emotional and social development.

Traditional bonding experiences, such as family game nights, outdoor playdates, and storytelling sessions, lay the foundation for strong relationships and communication skills. These activities encourage children to express themselves, understand non-verbal cues, and develop empathy as they engage with others in real-world scenarios. Parents can make a conscious effort to prioritize these experiences, setting aside dedicated time each week for family interactions without screens to ensure that children are not overly reliant on technology for entertainment.

At the same time, technology can enhance bonding experiences when used thoughtfully. Educational apps and interactive games can serve as excellent tools for families to connect and collaborate. For instance, playing a cooperative game together on a tablet can foster teamwork and problem-solving skills, while also allowing parents to guide their children's tech usage. By choosing age-appropriate technology that encourages participation and communication, caregivers can create shared experiences that enrich family dynamics.

To effectively balance screen time and outdoor play, it is advisable to establish clear boundaries regarding technology use. Setting limits on daily screen time and incorporating tech-free zones or times within the household can help cultivate an environment where traditional bonding activities thrive. Encouraging children to engage in physical activities, creative arts, and imaginative play not only counteracts the sedentary nature of excessive screen time but also strengthens family bonds through shared experiences and memories.

Ultimately, navigating the digital playground requires a thoughtful approach that respects both the benefits of technology and the irreplaceable value of traditional bonding experiences. By consciously integrating tech and face-to-face interactions, caregivers can equip children with the skills they need to navigate their social worlds effectively, both online and offline. This balanced approach not only fosters healthy relationships among family members but also ensures that children develop into well-rounded individuals capable of thriving in both the digital and physical realms.

## Using technology to enhance communication and connection

In the journey of introducing technology to young children, the focus should be on using it as a tool to enhance communication and connection rather than merely as a source of entertainment. Technology, when thoughtfully integrated into daily routines, can foster meaningful interactions among family members and peers. For instance, video calls can bridge the gap between family members who live far away, allowing children to maintain relationships with grandparents or cousins. Engaging in these conversations can help children develop important social skills, such as turn-taking and active listening, while also giving them a sense of belonging and connection to their extended family.

Moreover, technology can facilitate collaborative learning experiences that encourage communication and teamwork among children. Educational apps and platforms often include features that allow children to work together on projects or play interactive games that require group participation. This not only reinforces their learning but also teaches them how to communicate effectively with their peers. By engaging in technology-based group activities, children can learn to express their ideas and negotiate roles, which are essential skills for their personal and academic growth.

As parents and caregivers, it is crucial to set boundaries around technology use to ensure that it complements rather than replaces face-to-face interactions. Establishing technology-free zones or times, such as during family meals or playtime, allows for uninterrupted communication and connection among family members. Additionally, modeling appropriate technology use can guide children in understanding when and how to engage with their devices responsibly. This balance helps to create an environment where technology serves as a facilitator of connection while still prioritizing personal interactions.

Incorporating technology into family bonding activities can also enhance the overall experience. Families can utilize apps or online resources to plan games or educational activities that everyone can participate in together. Whether it's a virtual trivia night or a shared digital storytelling project, these activities can strengthen family ties while teaching children valuable skills such as cooperation and creativity. By making technology a part of shared experiences, parents can create lasting memories while demonstrating the positive aspects of tech use.

Lastly, teaching digital literacy from an early age is vital in ensuring that children understand the importance of communication and connection in the digital world. Parents can introduce concepts such as respectful online communication, the significance of privacy, and the importance of critical thinking when consuming digital content. By equipping children with these skills, they will be better prepared to navigate their digital playground safely and responsibly, ultimately leading to a more connected and engaged generation.